To Jules, with love – and thanks
for all your support and encouragement
Jan xxxx

BEYOND
PARADISE

c r o c u s

C

c r o c u s

BEYOND PARADISE

poetry by lesbians and gay men

First published in 1990 by Crocus

Crocus books are published by
Commonword Ltd,
Cheetwood House,
21 Newton Street,
Manchester M1 1FZ.

Commonword gratefully acknowledges financial assistance from the
Association of Greater Manchester Authorities, North West Arts Association
and Manchester City Council.

Typeset and printed by RAP Ltd, Rochdale, OL12 7AF.

British Library Cataloguing in Publication Data
Beyond paradise: poetry by lesbians and gay men.
    1. Poetry in English. Homosexual writers, 1945 —
    Anthologies
    I. Title
    821.9140809206

ISBN 0 946745 75 7

Contents

Introduction

The poetry you are about to read explores life and love with a vitality fitting for the new decade! The poems often concentrate on love — the one absolute that can affect each individual in a unique way: emotional and physical communion between two people has been celebrated since poets started writing. The wealth of original metaphor in *Beyond Paradise* highlights romance — and reality — in relationships. Compare, for example, the evocative description in 'Seaside Sunset', where a woman dreams of being with her lover, to the contrasting 'Rent', where ghetto boys are forced to sell themselves...But *Beyond Paradise* also shows how the effects of a relationship can spill out of the domestic arena; how lifestyles can become profoundly affected by sexuality. We see this in such poems as the gentle 'He and Me', which echoes a widely felt concern about the undemocratic Section 28.

Beyond Paradise offers a mixed dish of emotional ingredients: sadness, happiness, loneliness, and togetherness. Settings range from scenes of everyday life, such as the back seat of a crowded bus in 'The Journey' to the exotic wind-blown Bolivian village of 'Esta Noche...'.

This book displays the writing of talented gay and lesbian poets living in the North West. With humour and hope, passion and pain, these writers are looking forward to a golden age of equality and recognition — beyond paradise.

Louise Ansari
Commonword

WHO NEEDS COMMAS ANYWAY?

Suzanne Batty

This springtime Sunday clutters my peace with
musclemen and daytrippers making the most of a
moment's leisure despite the serrated edge of a
sea-breeze that raises my skin in chicken-flesh
bumps. My mother says long distance that
blizzards have closed Snake Pass but I say
blizzards what's blizzards? I'd leave this
sunshine salt-air to breathe that suffocating
snow-air to breathe the same air as you.
I'd like to tramp the frozen hills and kiss
your frozen lips hands ears anything would do.
I wish you were here with me now bruising our
bodies on the pebbles sharing a spliff or
two I'd slip an innocent hand beneath your
less than innocent shirt and show those hets
a thing or two. Act our age or less than. Age
now there's a thought my knees have wrinkles
I notice I'm no spring chicken quarter of a
century and none the wiser still wanting
everything all at once still wanting to
know what I'm capable of with you.

LAST WEEKEND

Hilary Bichovsky

Last weekend I inflated a huge idea of you
With a hand-pump, little gusts of air like the coughing of
   a cat
And floated it over Manchester.
You could have seen it there
Against the skyline, with the clouds.

That idea has come down, darling.

I SAW YOU

Hilary Bichovsky

I saw you looking at me,
Twice at an aspect of me
You could not ignore.

Once: my hand rests on my bike,
I make an exit, you
Kept your blue eyes on my ring,
Its past and presence fascinated you.

Twice: the morning of your sad message,
Me still drowsy on the bed,
Speaking solemnly you watched all the time
A delicate constellation of moles
On my arm.

Even while you said No,
You couldn't look away.

EXTRACT FROM 'REMEMBER'

Judith Bowers

Study, first make brain tick over,
feels hard getting back into clover.
Big success, pass law and physics,
paper enough to silence the critics,
to bolster an ego that's broken and shattered,
using school to discover what mattered.

College woman, still unsure,
knows enough to doubt the pure,
those who want to do good works
now just look like blinkered burks.
But stronger, certain sense of self,
one of the women above the shelf.

Back to the naive, innocent child,
soul still needs water, crashing, wild,
but now knows love, tender, kind,
not just love that twists the mind.
Often needs reminding, in dubious tones,
Life isn't all sand and stones.

COMING OUT

Cora Greenhill

In there was a simplicity
of skin over bone
desire returning home
that allowed a wealth
of metaphor

so I remember
a night of petals enfolding
unfolding a mystery
of stems and stamens
stirring a quiet riot
of limbs and hair
while tongues and hands and words slipped
everywhere
Eastern music hummed among our thighs
and a spasmodic tabla supplied
only the most obvious of our many rhythms

I remember too
how when we surfaced
our faces were still our own
but cleaner
more radiant

out here the full light of day exposes
a rougher riot of sun wind and water
the dangerous exuberance of an equinox storm
tumbling
the well-dressed earth

I would stride out and shout about
our naked loving to the windy air
scatter proprieties like branches in a gale

while the hills stand back
shocked
in their winter tweeds
but looking cleaner
more radiant.

INAMORATAS

Judith Bowers

I change, yet I still am the same,
same face, same body, same wit.
Some notice the change, some care
some don't so I remain, I sit,
constant, available, unable to move,
stifled, or shackled, by some sort of concern
because unlike others I still want to learn.
I recognise my changes, the changes of others
can easily be seen through observant eyes,
not the eyes of acquaintances, or mothers,
but through those of lovers.

I LEAVE EARLY IN THE MORNING

Cathy Bolton

I leave early in the morning,
Cycle through the damp, grey streets,
The smell of you still clinging
Like wet clothes to my skin.

I sit all day in an office,
Trapped in conversations which exclude me,
I smell you on my fingers and smile,
Bewildered, they return my smile.

Alone at night
The quilt reminds me,
I think of you in another part of the city
Cocooned in the same fragrance.

DRY-SHOD ACROSS YESTERDAY

Helen Smith

Today I walk dry-shod across yesterday's splashing ooze
Black mud frozen and black leaves crisped by frost
Between the saplings whose mute fingers praise the sky.

Days like this used to bond our love so neatly
Our smiles matched, we loved each other better for
   loving a day together
Garlands of arching rosehips congratulated our
   togetherness.

The ice on the ponds is patterned like the reeds that lie
   along the fringe
Beyond are the willows, smudged by the faint mist
Beyond again the road roars dimly, lorry windows
   semaphoring shiny messages.

The dog cracks the ice and stirs the mud
Bounds past the landmarks of the great flat valley
While I feed frosty beauty to my solitary joy.

'DO ME A FAVOUR...'

Mark Buckley

Scented snatches of conversations
Need the glowing tips of
Cigarettes — perfect —
In smoky bars and
Dance-floor sidelines.
The dark clubland's
Drugs to disguise
The delicate lips of potential
Lovers.
Brushed thighs
The crucial strike
The offered light —
'slike sex.

(Giving it up could really cramp my style)

There's comfort in a war
Where longing turns to lust
And frantic eyes search the rims
of rooms in smoky bars
No more friendly feel or the delicious
And sensual appeal of the one that's shared
No more now,
Voyager under the stars.

No more the smoker's restraint
Just me and the world —
The smoky bars
The dance-floor sidelines
Of the dark clublands
Who knows what may happen.

Christ! What will I do with my hands?

FOR ROSE

Pat Winslow

Sundays we split up and
Mondays you call me
to say
let's reconsider.

But this time it was for real
and now I have to pull myself up
by the bootstraps
and say it's over.

No hard feelings we say.
Still the best of friends.
We kiss
but don't make up

because there is no making up
left to do. We are still at last.
Free from
this crazy dance we do.

One step forward and two steps back.
One wanting whilst the other looks away.
And all the time
it's you, it's me

who does the hurting, who does the needing,
neither of us quite getting it
right.
We always seemed

to miss. How sad, we say,
to throw our seven years
on the heap
along with everybody else's.

How bitter to realize that we
were not so special after all.
We succumbed
just like the rest.

But no hard feelings.
Still the best of friends.
This, we say,
makes us different.

No recriminations and no
jealous tantrums either.
I own
and you own

nobody. We are the two boots
you once wrote to me about
in a poem —
laced together

but not so tightly that we
could not undo the knot.
And I love you
for that. For your practicality

and your humane respect.
There are no hard feelings. But
there is
pain over the

unexpectedness of little pieces of paper
which I find when I am working
alone.
Forgotten messages which say

hello, I love you, PTO —
tassles! and a little smiling face
drawn in biro
which I find in my dressing-gown pocket.

Or yesterday, when I was looking through
some poems and came across a card.
Happy
sixth train anniversary it said.

I don't cry over these things.
I cry when I can't get my
laces undone
at night. And I cry

when my period starts
because it reminds me of
who I am
and how little I was

when I first became a woman.
It's silly, but I miss you all the time
even though
we share the same house.

Best of friends sleeping in
separate beds like we did before.
But
this is for real now

I keep telling myself. And I don't
pretend or hope. I won't
allow it.
We'll keep both sides of the bargain

like we said. And we'll find other
more satisfactory ways of
learning
to live with each other —

my life,
        my love,
                my friend.

SCOTS PINE

Nawal Gadalla

I used only to go after
anything in trousers.
But now I've broadened my outlook,
and there's a special providence
in the fall of a kilt.

YOUR FACE, MY HEART

Monika Montsho

I saw a face today
Which reminded me of the place
Where I first met you
Which reminded me of the time
We first spoke
And my heart was already yours
In cold alleyways and doorways
On park benches and hotel floors
That time was ours
The world stood still
And I tattooed your name on my heart

I saw a face today
Which reminded me
That when you left and took your things
You also took a piece of my heart.

CIRCLING

Tommy Barclay

Politics, the weather,
Going away this year?
The unavailability
Of a decent pint of beer.
Last night's television,
The threatened transport strike.
That's my point exactly,
We're very much alike.

Problems with the neighbours,
Antics with the mates.
Sod this bloody council,
Have you seen the rates?
This is more like music,
Makes today's sound tame.
Funny you should like it,
Our taste must be the same.

Tales about the workmates,
Complaints about the car.
Do your drinking local?
Got a favourite bar?
Random conversation,
Couldn't be less planned.
Circling, circling, circling,
Till it's clear to land.

ACROSS THE HALLWAY

Jan Freeman

Across the hallway
the wind blows gently
through the open window.
Your denim jacket
lies strewn across unmade bed
the five a.m. rush to the airport.

Memories of that 'night-before'
your drunken state, your bawdy jokes,
'holiday toyboys'
'get your Durex from a toilet machine'
— your sexual intentions
making my love seem so obscene.

Across the hallway
a perfumed hint
we were lovers
mingles still on crumpled pillows.
Lying in the arms of another
I heal, I soothe, memories fade...

DANIEL'S SONG

Christopher Watt

Together we ignore the alarm
Tug the sheets
And link our arms
I race you for the Shredded Wheat
You take the water's precious heat
And splash at me with naked feet
And gently-grasping palms

Jeremy is twenty-three
He lives with me
I love him and he loves me
But we are just pretending

You call me in the afternoon
Arrange to eat
And I'll see you soon
Insisting on avoiding meat
You laugh and choose a window seat
And join our eyes in the evening's heat
And a soft-remembered tune

Jeremy is twenty-three
He eats with me
I love him and he loves me
But we are just pretending

I link my hand with your fingers
Climb the stairs
And linger
The touch of you is like a dare
The laying of each other bare
And sharing this will surely tear
The song from love the singer

Jeremy is twenty-three
He sleeps with me
I love him and he loves me
And we are not pretending

CUT FREE

Tommy Barclay

There was a time
When the memory of you
Was a blade.
Sharp, gleaming,
Slicing through everyday thoughts
And deeds.
Pinning my mind to the past
With a sudden
Stab of longing.
Or piercing simple pleasure
To impale the bud of joy.

Now,
The cutting-edge is dull.
It marks,
But draws no blood.
The stiletto-point
Is blunted.
In time
Your memory will be sheathed.
And my healing heart
Will cease
To be your whetstone.

SOME MORE ABOUT ROSES

Mark Buckley

We are planting the roses together.
I dig the holes in appropriate places
While you gently remove those other forms,
'They are in the way', you persist,
Replanting them elsewhere.
The roses, from a friend, are old,
But they will be fine you say,
And show me how to tell the colour of the flower
By the colour of the leaves.
I try to remember what you tell me
But I realise that I don't really care.
Your hands.
My heart.
This moment.

OLD LOVE

Sarah Corkhill

How to tell, how to confess my change
We lower our expectations of ourselves
And let the physical go
It happened a long time ago, feels like ancient lovers
Sleeping together, hugging either side of the bed
Barely a good night between us.
Are we what becomes of all good love?
Have we lived out the human bond?
Should we try harder
Make a clean break
Or try it on someone else?

BREAST

Sarah Corkhill

You showed me where your breast had been
I wanted to see a pink star
Or at least a medical pattern
But all I saw was your womanhood hacked at.
When you said you had always had young girl's breasts
I wanted to weep in a megaphone
For you and the possibility
Of the poisoning in us all
But instead I kissed your scar.
You walk tall and straight no less of yourself
And I pray it won't keep you from hugs and lovers
Most precious death defying flaw
To even now live as if forever.

FACE

Sarah Corkhill

Looking at your face,
Leaning into your shoulders
I see the grey teasing the blonde
The thick arched brows
Frown into a discerning stare
Blue eyes that push away
And can suddenly wink and daredevil
Thin, broad lips pushing forward the point
The hungry, sharp teeth
And stubborn, handsome jaw.

Looking for too long at your tigerish, freckled skin,
The dimples, the down, the half-closed eyes,
I am hallucinating on the possibility
Of everlasting buzz...
That recurring cerebral wet dream
That makes one hand
Hold down the other,
Unable to test it yet.

PICTURESQUE HEARTS

P. D. Cookson

Clear blue summer days
Daffodils in wind
Ducks quacking
Seem a thousand miles away
To the two boys on the park bench
Looking at each other's
Golden faces
A man is picking roses
For a wife who
Lies in a hospital bed
But Mike and John
Don't notice other
People's lives

Neither touches lunch
in this special moment
They go home
A little later
Two boys with
Perfect alibis
And picturesque hearts

HOW DARE YOU?

Sarah Corkhill

I have told my mother I prefer women
And introduced my lover to my father
I explained to my sisters why I have no boyfriend.
I have tormented myself through a year-long affair at school
Only to tell friends later who never guessed
And now I reprimand pupils for anti-gay slogans.
I have challenged my bosses' queer-bashing laughter
And had an affair with a woman
Only four years younger than my mother.
On stage I have declared my tendencies
Riddled out my inclinations in poems, jokes and cabaret
In public I have worn the badges, sung the songs
And kissed the forbidden.
I have discussed *The Color Purple* with a nun at school,
Speculated on the lesbian behaviour of my tortoiseshell cat
And advertised a lesbian room.
Happily I have perpetuated our collective madness
Until I came to you.
We have grown very close with all this bloody telepathy
Your approval or rejection teetering on that knife edge
So powerful I have swallowed twenty-seven years of personal
    progress.

How dare you tongue-tie me you smug, celibate temptress.

RENT

P. D. Cookson

Corner of the streets
Down to the last
Cigarette of the week
He plays the game
Of give to me baby
This sex in a ghetto
Where a fiver means maybe
And he answers no
To every second question
asked
Death is unmasked

Behind closed doors
The punters seek more
Than just a night in bed
And a mess on the floor
And somewhere in
Red-light midnight strikes
And blue and white
Paper pictures of
Her Majesty the Queen
Are exchanged for lust
From the kerb crawl Volvos
This is shit or bust
And he'll go through it all again
Tomorrow and tomorrow and tomorrow

HER DOCS

Pat Winslow

Boots
striding out boots
echoing down the road.
A solitary figure
in a solitary blackness
with her chin in her scarf
and her scarf in her jacket
layer
upon
layer
of protection.
Head held high boots
hard and shiny on the outside
soft and supple on the inside
wrinkling with age
and springy as the first day
she bought them.
Knotted high up the ankle
they hold her
tight
firm
and steady
make her feel
unyielding
and at the same time
protect her precious bones within.
Dyke boots
that are polished
lovingly
every night.
The quick dab of black
and the kiss of a brush

against strong leather
searching out the creases
and always finding them.
Then the final crowning glory
of the cloth
sliding
back and forth
over toe
heel
and sides
revealing
the gleaming object of desire
in its state of grace.
Proud boots.
Out and proud.
Her Docs
were the first trappings
of her chosen identity
the first acknowledgement
of her growing vulnerability
and the last statement (she thought)
in street credibility.
She will have them
till she's seventy
she says
though by then
she hopes to have
a leather jacket as well.

JACK-IN-THE-BOX

Cathy Bolton

'I'm a Lesbian.'
My words take you by surprise.

'But you've been out with men,
You can't be a real Lesbian!'
Your words come as no surprise.

You see me spring up overnight,
But I grew up quietly, in the dark.
My roots run deep,
They feed me strength
To carry your disapproval.

HAWERBY HALL

Cora Greenhill

In the conservatory — 1

On a sofa plummy as labia
a woman is curled —
a fragile reflection caught in a bubble.

In the conservatory — 2

Walls softly surfaced as lullabies
chairs moss-green, touch-pink, love-gilded,
the garden seen through glass in April's aura.

Outside

The flat earth is ploughed with razors,
square fields are lurid with rape.
A Red Arrow unzips the screaming sky.

In the bath

Green bath — full, warm and frothy,
my flesh spreads, limb-lazy, resting,
like a Maltese Goddess, drowning.

THE JOURNEY

Tommy Barclay

A summer Saturday, a crowded bus.
I read, for the fourth time,
The same dense paragraph of my magazine.
Around me, snatches of the usual bus-ride topics...
The weather...crowded shops...bus service...last night's
    telly.
Then I see you, standing somewhat unsteadily in the aisle
As the driver enjoys his favourite game of
    stop...shudder...go.
Our eyes meet, and I move nearer the window
Thus creating a narrow but inviting space
Between me and the kid with his nose in a *Masters of the
    Universe* comic.
Bless these long back seats.
You smile gratefully. I nod acknowledgement and turn,
With sudden great interest, to the sunny and thronged
    streets.
You arrange your rather up-market carrier bags
On the floor between your feet and on your lap.
The heat is oppressive, the bus windows closed tight.
This being England, passengers would sooner melt or
    complain
Than be dashingly vulgar enough to open a window.
Luckily, you and I are wearing short-sleeved shirts.
Sitting close, because of the crush, of course,
Our arms touch.
Our bare arms.
Skin on skin.
I feel the tensing of your muscles.
Or is it mine?
But you do not move.
You could.
I could.
But we don't.

POPPIES

Christopher Watt

A pale blue parasol, tilted back
Behind a loosely-ribboned hat.
A smaller figure walks beside
Deeper in the sweeping field.

Yes mother, but this is not a very good print;
The poppies are not red enough.

Further back, on the slope of the bank
A darker dress, another pair.
The trees rise in their rear,
Spread to the peeping house.

I awake at ten, alone.
Ah, the rules of course — a chance to leave.

The colour reaches forward,
Flowers rippling through the grasses,
Shadows falling luxuriously
Amongst the light.

Quietly I pick for my clothes.
And there is Monet again. Another wall.
I do not need to switch on the light;
I know the poppies are not red enough.

IN THE PROCESS

Di Williams

When I say I am fêted as a writer,
I do not mean, photographed,
on page seven of the Advertiser,
book in hand, near the champagne;
I do not mean, fetid like cheese;
nor fated, to leave all other paths
and die a starving writer in a garret —
that would be fatal —
no; rather say I am foet-id,
like a foetus, I am created,
like a pregnant woman I create.
I incubate
in the warm fluids of imagination
the primitive tissues
which will form a new entity
and give it birth and a name.
Fait accompli.

NEW DANGER

Sarah Corkhill

I wince at how quickly you throw yourself at men
Your strength and independence vanish.
How could you forget yourself?

Slowly, slowly we have moved together wary and restrained
I cannot help ask if we'll move closer still.
To what? Physical love?
Too loaded to risk a mistake
To erase all the verbal confessions,
The swopping of flaws, scar to scar
We are still not sure we won't be rejected
We won't demand, be demanded of too much.
Not sure enough to rub the aching shoulder
That shelters the throbbing chest
Not sure enough to kiss the scar
And call it beautiful.

I wince at how quickly I throw myself at you
My strength and independence vanish.
How could I forget myself?

HE AND ME

P. D. Cookson

We like to go to cafes
And have cakes and tea
He and me

We like to go to Blackpool
And gaze at the sea
He and me

We like to demonstrate
For our equality
He and me

We like to declare
Our homosexuality
He and me

We would like to
Hold hands publicly
He and me

But that kind of affection
Is not reality
For he and me

Most of all
We'd like to believe
That there's no such thing
As Section 28
In a democracy
He and me

SKIN AGAINST SKIN

Helen Smith

I am leaning against a black brick wall
Waiting for a bus
To take me drinking
With a woman I have known for years.
She came home with me after last week's disco
She has large mushroom-coloured nipples.

The slugs are leaving the parapet of the black wall,
Lowering themselves on a silken rope
Which they hold in their mouths.
Their bodies shimmer
For a moment they swing aimlessly in space
Their bodies twisted one around the other.

They are pushing against and around each other now,
Which sends them spinning under the pink fluorescent
    street lights.
They are equal reflections, eagerness making rhythm.
They are sinuous caresses
Closer then interleaved knees
More familiar than tongue on cunt.

The hand-pump swoops down on the river of beer,
I am late for my date but explain about the slugs,
Demonstrate with my fingers, persuade with my voice,
Fail to shift the disbelief from her face.
At eleven she is surprised that I am going home alone,
Withdraws her disdain; I think about the mushrooms.

The wall above the bar is mirrored
Our reflections tarnished.
Could we absorb the cool earthen smells from each other?

Would our skins whisper against skin like the sea on
    the strand?
My bus snakes its way home across the city motorways
I catch sight of her sulking in a doorway. No.

PRIVATE CELEBRATIONS

Cathy Bolton

Hidden from the public eye,
Away from those curious fists
And spitting tongues
We'll celebrate our love.

To dark rooms
We'll take a candle and some wine
And celebrate our love.

To quiet mountainsides
We'll take a rainsheet and cigarettes
And celebrate our love.

In select bars
With knowing glances, and some restraint
We'll celebrate our love.

At private readings
With bitter poems in angry words
We'll celebrate our love.

PEACHES

Cora Greenhill

when I receive your very gentle
love
on a postcard full of flowers
my tears burst like hailstones
that suddenly pelt the earth
to melt at once in this
sun-soaked spring

for our efforts to meet
were long opposed
by the camps
we carried inside us
and by neglected frightened
little natives of our persons
who set traps
shot darts sideways
from the thickets

but now we have swallowed the silk-salt sweetness
inside the slate of the oyster
we've licked the soft slush
from the gooseberry
and from the syrup of our soft interiors
poems are pouring like peaches from a tin.

LATE AFTERNOON

Simon Bailey

The glass butterfly turns
across the sunlight of late afternoon,
to and fro.

Thus you turn for me,
with light that fractures through you,
late, but not extinguished yet.

PAS DEVANT LES ENFANTS

Judith Bowers

Mysteriously
    make love
hug kiss feel dream
    or hate
punch kick hurt scream,
But,
not in front of the children!

Indulgently,
embrace the warmth of another
sharing
the love of a sister or brother
But,
not in front of the children.

Yet astoundingly,
    make war,
kill burn rape maim,
    nation
or state, still it's the same
But,
Pas devant les enfants?

GLASTONBURY CIRCLE DANCE WEEK, FEBRUARY 1986

Nawal Gadalla

i fell in
love with you
as i watched you dance
across the circle.
sometimes, outside it, i'd
sit one out to watch you,
to register a growing core
one that started in my belly and
rose to my throat...(feeling deep
and words to speak).
i saw your elegance, head bowed,
delicate foot pointing,
containment, certainty,
poise and beauty,
movement.
and a femininity so frail
i wanted to look away to
divert myself as though
i'd witnessed a taboo.
i shall see you, and
across a circle
maybe still throw a
shy and sideways
glance
that holds you
as you dance.

NIGHT-TIME IS DIFFERENT

Nic Collins

Night-time is different.
Just darkness and you, and you
a finger away.
No breath left now,
silence, sticky and slow.
Aware now, of my pins and needles,
my head against the wall.
Your arm beneath my neck,
stubble against my cheek,
The sheet, half off,
half on.
Night-time is different
your mouth, around my ear,
unbearable pleasure.
Oh yes.
Night-time is different.

Daytime now.
I've left breadcrumbs on the board,
the seat, up.
Not wrung the cloth out,
the door, open,
the light, on.
Shopping was awful.
I've managed to annoy you in
ten new ways.
I try to keep up
with your changes of mood.
I'm breathless with tact
I tiptoe and stamp.
It's like running after a
mad March hare

that I don't really
want to catch,
not now,
oh no.
Not until night-time.
Night-time is different.

JUST FRIENDS

Cora Greenhill

I say
I've got over you   when
I've slipperysoaped your skin   found
your mouth in a stream of water   watched
the bubbling well between our four breasts
again

when we have dried each other's thighs
and you say   that's far enough
and I throw down the towel   and suddenly
we're kissing   and throwing
fire down each other's throats
again

I say
I've got over you   because
I can happily be with you   loving
the light way our limbs plait
themselves together on the sofa
like cats   in front of my fire   as we talk
for hours   forgetting
to eat   until
it's so late we decide to share
my bed with our T-shirts
on   and tampons in   still
just
        friends

and all night it seems
I dream of you
in your fine new house
as I spill shoeboxes

of my past
on your floor
crying with frustration
without
      being
           heard

OUR SORT

Russell Morris

We men are counterfeit in your eyes;
We walk touch and breathe much the same
Or do we?
We take our hands and hold them
When we can.
We understand a truth in skin
Like yourselves.

But our truths have been forced within piss-stained walls,
Our last refuge,
Our commonground
With you.

There we score those tiles with lust and a key,
Fill tender to flooding the chamber with our voice of brass
    teeth.
Or in fear
And your fear too,
We muffle
Our dribbles in our flesh-filled mouths.

Because of you we love
And we have loved here
In our water-filled shrine.

We take a chance
For a love of our sort,
Or a persecution
For our rite
And your conscience.

FOR YOU

P. D. Cookson

Silver bells
That toll for you
Sweet smell
Of the red rose for you

Bright lights
That spell your name for you
Best nights
Playing love games with you

Autumn leaves
Dried and pressed for you
Ali Baba and his thieves
Stealing the best for you

Folk songs
Of ancient days for you
Few long weekends
Spent far away with you

Poems and prose
Of unrequited love for you
All my last Rolos
I could give up for you

Gift-wrapped
And presented straight to you
Sit in my lap
For I can't wait for you

All this and more
I could give to you
If you would only walk through the door
I wonder if you ever will do

PLOUGHSHARES AND BALLERINAS

Jan Freeman

The lapping waves on the seashore
through the night...

In the morning I wake up, beside you,
strained in my gut.
What do I do now?
I creep from the bed
and peep through the curtain;
the sea hangs grey under big cloud.
The old man in the field
is fixing the thick horse to the ploughshare.
Some people know how to live
day to day with meaning.

You call my name softly;
do you still know me?
'What are you doing?
Come back to bed.'
I slip back under the sheets
and lie stiff against the edge.
'You're acting as though
you've never seen me before.'
Puzzled, you reach out
your hand and stroke down my arm.
Frozen, I watch the ceiling;
an opera house is filling,
old ladies with binoculars
watch the ballerinas on stage...

If I wasn't such a Bohemian
I wouldn't have slept with you last night.

SEAN

Christopher Watt

Three days gone:
And you settle on my mind
A foot in the door
But I pushed, I pushed
And the stupidity of it was, I knew.
I do this every time:
A conversation
The door is compromised
The walls fall down
And my imagination is loosed:

'I clutch a ticket to Manchester
Or wait on the station at Hull
I wrap you in my arms
But of course it's a load of bull
Five days gone:
And we've been together for months
I know you don't like radishes
And have never had the mumps
Seven days gone:
Our anniversary's here
We both buy Lloyd Cole LPs
And fool around the pier
Eight days gone:
I tell you that it's love
But you don't seem to want to know
And have I seen your gloves?'

Three days gone:
And I don't know what to do
I should have spoken
But the walls were warm and wet
And the crowd was thick and fast
I should have spoken
But neither did you...did you?

VALENTINE'S DAY

Monika Montsho

This morning
I woke up ready
To count my
Valentine cards.
One finger was enough.
I even emptied the
Bin
The night before
In preparation for all
The envelopes I was to discard
Cleared the mantelpiece
For my new card collection
But I should have known that
One magpie couldn't lie
That one finger was
Perfectly adequate
No waste-paper bin required.

THE SEDUCTION

Tommy Barclay

Where can I turn from the frank,
                    blue-eyed stare of you?
The hand slowly pushed through the thick,
                    sun-blond hair of you.
Be brave and be strong and be sure
                    to beware of you.
But how to escape from the
                    so-tempting snare of you.

Where can I hide from the slick,
                    no-shit style of you?
The bold tongue that glosses the smart,
                    up-front smile of you.
Be cool and be calm and ignore
                    the profile of you.
Pretend not to notice the sheer
                    laid-back guile of you.

Yet why should I run from this deep,
                    long-felt need in me?
This yearning that moves with a strange,
                    wound-up speed in me.
Deny and defy what could help love
                    succeed in me.
When one smile could lead to my soul
                    new-born, freed in me.

SLEEPING SIDEWAYS

Nic Collins

Sleeping sideways.
Imperial now.
We've left old money behind,
gone decimal.
Our relationship
is metric.
Third cousins, twice removed,
nephews and nieces
write:
'To you both'
and:
'Love always x'
Accepted?
maybe,
Happy?

But, no toasters,
sets of towels, decanters
or sherry glasses.
No stainless steel pans,
No bottom drawer
No 'do you take this man?'
or 'till death do us part'
Till death.

Till death do we hide?
It's still old money,
the bad penny.
Always turning up in
feet and inches,
metres and centimetres
it means the same.

We live, together.
We share a life.
That's A1.
Big size.
No half measure,
it's cubic all the way.

So you can keep your tumble drier,
your matching kettle and
toasted sandwich maker.
All your gifts
of security.
That's your life,
your religion,
we're sleeping sideways.

SEASIDE SUNSET

Suzanne Batty

a slow globe sun
sighs, sets, sinks with
a shiver.
another seaside sunset, with
the rubbish and romantics,
down by this sewage sea.
this town feels like my mind,
all lovepeaceandunderstanding —
a junkyard underneath.
idle thoughts strung out like
sea front lights like a string of
pearls
like a rosary;
everything comes back to you.

for example.

this sky is like your eyes —
like night like flames like the
Blue John caves.
I could say I'd give up
mountains (well, I would)
just to hold your hands,
long sweet gentle hands
that curl against me
like a flower.
I wonder what your hands
are doing now?
I wish I was your coffee cup
your half-smoked cigarette.

four in the morning.

I think my fingernails have
grown since I saw you last;
my hair's grown shorter.
I've seen four in the morning
with a Silkcut and The Smiths
far more times than I'd
care to admit.
my bed just smells of me these days
all bad dreams and restless nights.
how are you sleeping? log-like? alone?
my paranoia grows with this miserable
half-light.

I want you.

it's neither here nor
there if you're here or
there, I still want you.
I want you soft and warm
I want your body your breath
trembling; I want to hold your
soul your heart your heat in
these hands; longing lonely
lustful hands that would
love you to exhaustion that would
love you till they're old if you'd
let them.

SLENDER THREAD

Jan Freeman

And as I feel your body
slip next to mine,
the coolness of the night
makes you move in
a little closer.

I tremble at your touch.
'Oh, you're cold,' you say
with your soft concern,
'let me warm you.'
Your hand rubs my shoulder.

My eyes search the darkness.
I have contrived every step, for you
to be here, next to me, tonight.
Now I am lost for manoeuvres.
The sound of your breath
makes me weak.

Shall I go to sleep,
exhausted by futility?
Shall I try yet one more time
to make us transcend
that fine hair's breadth line
between friends and lovers.

I turn gently on my side
and curl softly against your back.
My fingers slide slowly into your palm
and grasp
your limp sleeping hand.

ESTA NOCHE SE PRODUCIRA UN ECLIPSE TOTAL DE LA LUNA

Suzanne Batty

'Esta Noche' sees us
searching the streets
for coffee or tea,
no easy task in this
windswept dust-blown town
where both water and
heat are in short supply.

Looking up from the
dusty piss-stained street
the sky opens out,
grazing the iron roofs and
already a thumbprint
shadows the moon.

So we take a side-street,
climb steep stone steps,
gasping cold thin air which
stabs my Marlboro-ed lungs.

That's all there is
between me and the stars,
cold thin dust-blown air.

Up on the monument
crowds of Bolivians with
telescopes and tripods
forget the desperation of
this life, this town, this
desolation. Death, dig yourself
down in this nothing dust,
we're looking to the
sky; we're looking to this

shadow which eats the moon
alive.
A girl flashes past, running
from railing to railing, crying
'La luna! La luna!'

I think I'm holding my breath
waiting for the lights to go out
or the end of the world or
something.

The city lights are
spread below us, a
sulphurous sheet that
curves away around the
earth. We're staring into
space, where fireworks like
fireflies glide, red, gold and
green, blinked out in this
ink-black night, and, above
us, this pyrotechnic dream.
I've never seen so many
stars, or known so few;
the Southern Cross, a
planet or two,
(I haven't seen the Llama yet),
and La Luna Rosa, flowering,
other-worldly.

In that other-worldly
world below us
adobe walls and corrugated
roofs rattle and hum as
Radio Bolivia blasts
Hip Hop House into the
breathless Altiplano wind
which whistles out across the
plains, stirring dust devils
and devilish dreams.

I wonder if you're looking too
from dear old Inglaterra, or
if you're sleeping with your
arm across your eyes
the way you used to.
I'm not surprised you guard them
I would too, hugging them to you
like a well-kept secret.
Your eyes would eclipse the moon
every night if I could
look into them just
once or twice.

If I close my eyes I can
reach across and curl my
fingers into yours,
turn your shadowed eyes to
stars that burn in the
silence we shared.
My sleeping self still
reaches for you, finds
nothing but dust and dreams
the distant memory of arms
and legs around me, my
lips against your sweet
soft sleeping skin.

WORD HAD IT

Jan Freeman

Word had it, they'd gone for a very good reason,
more words said they'd been caught in the long grass,
one lying on top of the other
as though she were a boy.

Word had it, they'd done well in the exams,
more words said they'd have made it to Oxford.
Doing wicked things like that
it was right they were expelled.

Years later I met them in the precinct,
trendy overcoats, side by side,
glancing at my uniform
'Ah, you're a prefect now',
the fair one smiled.

I sit by the long grass,
wishing hard I wasn't alone.
The fair one stoops to kiss me
then pushes me down.
Down, down in the long grass
her on top — it feels like home.

Word has it I'm going to Oxford,
more words say I'm going alone.

THE LOCK

Russell Morris

Oh they move about and they weave about
In this dull little house.
The touch of wet fingers on somebody's lips
The sound of warm skin, hip against hip.
Muffled noise and assertion...
Of love
For candlewax, lemon oil and liqueur sweetened breath.

Oh they move about and weave about,
Leave their salted and colourless trails
In tissues, balled tight,
Tight as clams holding pearls.

Yet they move about and weave about
But no memory of you escapes...
Through this lock on my door.

RESTAURANT

Jan Freeman

Run from the car
across busy main road
into the restaurant.
Pause at the door,
take a breath.
She's sat in the corner,
chiselled profile absorbed
in a Greek village painting.
For this moment
I am free
of her,
our entanglements,
the problems.
She sucks, sultry, on her cigarette,
a natural pout
any film director
would like to capture.
She blows her inhalation
out,
so sensuous.
I feel rapture.
She is waiting for me
but all I bring is
words I don't want to say.
The waiter fills her glass,
sets the wine on the table.
Turning,
I push the door
and cross
the busy main road.

YOU LOOKED AT ME THIS MORNING

Pat Winslow

You looked at me this morning
and you said I was wasting away.
And not understanding
why I should feel so defensive about it
you happened to remark
God! I wish I was thin,
as if missing someone
and wishing you no longer had to drag your body around
were some kind of goal to be attained.

I watch you daily
filling up on soft looks and tender postcards,
taking your share of the caresses
from both of us.
And I go hungry
needing you, and wanting you
to nurture me back to how I was.
But how I was is gone now
and going back is just a longing I have.

There are only so many parts
that can fit together
and once a piece is lost
then it is gone forever.
If I miss you with my body
then I'm sorry,
I can't help it.
It wasn't on purpose that I
shrank to make you feel fatter.

UNDER MOONLIGHT AND LINEN

Russell Morris

His uncovered torso, without knowledge
Accepts a triangle of light,
From a new moon above a street of strange names.

This is a gift passed through the meeting of curtains
To a kouros in rest.

Slowly this light will journey from rib to rib
Until, it reaches a place where white linen flows in
     folds.
Here the sculptor's touch is veiled from the light.
Unseen are the marble veins and stylized hair
Unknown his sensuous, his guileful skill.

But once,
Like a lover from ancient Greece
I wrote a message with my tongue upon this thigh.
Its moisture remains
Under moonlight and linen.

THE WET WEEKEND

Toby Manning

Here in England
all it ever does is rain;
beating at the unripe pears
that fall in cascades with the
birds upon the sodden earth outside.

He entertains me —
takes me out walking through the
mud and water lilies,
apple trees and streams
and rising weeds amid the water.
Then, he whistles to his dog
and obediently we follow.

It rained all weekend,
he just back from sun and sea
and me fished out to
while away the ordered hours.
But I just followed as
the streets wound round themselves
and my conversation
turned and stared me in the face,
and it embarrassed both of us.

We went out to the briny seas of England,
drank lukewarm tea,
and sickened ourselves on sticky cakes.
And as we walked along the quay
the rain seemed only to soak me,
as we stared out to all that
lay across the gravy sea.

One night I dreamed about
a boy upon a dolphin,
turning cart-wheels through
the waves and streaming light that
ran across his flickering body
laughing, untouched, and lithe
as the salt ran and dried
in my dream.

Back in England
all it did was rain
soaking into me
dragging my clothes across
my narrow frame
until my steps were heavy with water,
until each pore and perforation
clogged.
And he walked on ahead
leaving me to carry the weight
of the wet weekend we shared.

THIEVES AND LOVERS

Russell Morris

In a whole city
A hundred streets, each with two names,
Through which our feet passed for a second time;
We saw our lovely facades
And we'd care for...we'd take.

A balcony was ours
Mock pillars, plaster fruit.
I cared for the roofscapes
Lifted your eyes,
Hoisted them skywards to the bolstering clouds;
To the spires and weather-vanes
And to the city's nerve endings.

Between raised finger and eye you claimed a verdigris
    needle,
Wagered war with Zeus,
Defied his lightning strikes.

Your charge ran to earth
Through gold wire and brocade, threading Hollywood
    breasts,
Encrusting shoulders,
Expensively sealed against thieves.
You stole their price-tags behind reinforced glass...
Just by looking.

In this city with two names
With you, whatever I saw I stole
For a second time.

At the junction of two roads
Albertinkatu Albertsgatan, Bulevardi Bulvarden;
We considered as thieves our next haul.
I looked, and my eyes were in yours.

As thieves we own what we see,
But just for that moment
I cast time as the criminal.
In a city with two names
Thieves and lovers are the same.

STRENGTH

Di Williams

Discovered by accident;
In the small woman who had been nestling in my crooked
    arm —
I picked her up and hugged her.
'Watch out! No one does that,
You're lucky I let you —'
Both of our bodies tense,
Mine in embarrassment.
I forget which colour belt my lover was,
Nearly a black belt, karate.
I do not remember relaxing after that day.

Or unintentionally;
I was feeling good,
A warm summer evening,
Uncurling in t'ai chi chuan
Because I felt good and grounded
Swept round, supple, went on
To the close.
Usually I did it alone, at home.
She told me a lot later
Not to flex my muscles
In her house,
As if I had been showing off.
I had only been celebrating.

Or incidentally;
As part of another kind of strength,
I lay in another woman's arms,
Completely safe, held,
While she told me,
'You need loving.'

Her back and shoulders carried people
Onto beds and wheelchairs all day,

And she had a lover of her own
To comfort when she rested.

I have not met my match.
I want a strength to answer,
The luxury of a woman concentrating
That fine skilled effort on me
While I, unthreatened, thrill to the challenge
And can feed back that strength,
A dialogue.

WAREHOUSE

Helen Smith

This warehouse overlooks the sea
Coming in we saw it high and red against the grey
We have been stood inside it, by a wall.
Here is a pebble trapped in a brick
It has burnt an explosion into the baked clay.
I trace smooth pebble, sharp burn, ridge of rasping mortar.

Into the dark maw of the warehouse comes the cotton.
Seedy white fibres that dragged me from my place
Now squared into sacking-wrapped bales.
Men paler than sailors, bigger, redder, whisk and haul.
We stumble out of their path, still expecting heaving boards.
I resist this new chill certainty.

We are more wares, still on our way.
'It'll be fancy where you're going,' said one of the sailors
Same as the merchant said,
'I fancy these three.'

He hand picked us. Judged us
Too fine for cotton-picking, for hand-picking
Which is back-breaking.
If picking me could break him...

I am the youngest of us three.
Between us there is still some reminder, some proof,
Some truth of the people and places far behind.
Yet there are hours when the others seem pale to me,
    thin-blooded
And in their eyes I see myself quiet too, and pale.
Three wraiths in our pallid cotton shifts.

'Better to be dead,' I think in these hours,
And slip back to my dream.
Green bubbles stream up past my wide eyes,
The welcome green bubbles from the deep of the sea.

FREE DANCE

Nawal Gadalla

ah women, come and dance with me
open a place inside and
gallop restlessly without the words that
hide you
be a kind daughter or be a
monstrous mother
but flee the dust which
claims you must
be either.

PRESCIENCE

Tommy Barclay

I do not yearn for other days,
Or other loves long gone.
There is no precise something
I can place my finger on.
I cannot point to this, or that,
No act do I regret.
Today is just like yesterday,
And yet, my love,
And yet...

I greet you with the same fond smile,
Your company still seek.
I can detect no wrong note,
No discord when we speak.
No shadow cast upon the sun,
There is no sense of threat.
Today is just like yesterday,
And yet, my love,
And yet...

Biographies

Simon Bailey
I find myself exploring two particular paths — spirituality and personal relationships. The one finds me searching through the world of religion, the other has led me to discover what it means to be gay. The two can conflict but the tension can be fruitful too.

Tommy Barclay
I'm six feet tall, incredibly handsome, built like a Greek god, and lie about my appearance. One day, when the literary world comes to its senses, I will be awarded a Pulitzer Prize and a brace of Bookers. Until then, I live modestly in Leigh practising my chat show repartee.

Suzanne Batty
I grew up in South Manchester and since then have been a hostel worker in London, suicidal in Sheffield, a sort of student dishwasher waitress cleaner gardener drummer rock-climber and in love in Brighton, and a climber of volcanoes in South America. I have been a poet for at least six months and a dyke for a lot longer.

Hilary Bichovsky
I am twenty-eight, anxious and city-bound — fighting a losing battle against the current wave of individualism. I am a member of Outlanders writing group. Three years ago I had my heart broken: may these poems lay that ghost to rest.

Cathy Bolton
Three years ago I moved to Manchester, came out as a lesbian and as a writer. Since then most of my poetry has been written to perform. I am a member of Outlanders (Manchester lesbian writers' group) and the Northern Dyke Writers. I have previously been published in *She Says* (Crocus) and *Thoughtprints* (Chorlton Women Writers).

Judith Bowers

Born in Preston, I am thirty-two years old, a mother and a feminist. Having served my apprenticeship to conventionality, I started writing to express my own personal experiences, differences, and anger. I owe much to the strength and support of the women that surround and astound me, especially Sandra, Sandy and Kay. I have a strong commitment to issues surrounding women and anti-discrimination based on gender, race and class.

Mark Buckley

I'm thirty years old and apart from three years in London — which I didn't particularly like — I've lived in Preston all my life. I don't think I'm an adventurous person and I'd like this to come out in my poetry. I dislike all rules which make my sexuality an issue. I dislike rules in general.

Nic Collins

August 24th 1963 — I was born, and grew up in Cumbria till eighteen. Briefly to London and back. Next a foundation course in Carlisle, on to a printed textile degree at Liverpool. Three more years being an artist — sometimes successfully. Now Manchester, another course, and up to date so far.

P. D. Cookson

This is P. D. Cookson. I was born in 1965 in Moss Side, Manchester and then moved to Heywood near Rochdale in 1970 where I lived until moving back to Manchester in 1984. I started writing in 1985 and have continued ever since. My work is, I like to think, rather eccentric but above all I think it represents the feelings of a lot of people I know. Good luck and stay beautiful.

Sarah Corkhill

Norfolk-born I home hopped France and the USA before returning to ancestral North, careering through Pretty Disgusting Things '82 — '85, co-ordinator of Manchester Women Live '85, '86, '87, and now writing with the Outlanders '88 — showcasing at The Green Room every International Women's Week: in between posing as teacher of English and drama.

Jan Freeman
Wrote my first serious novel when I was eight and that fired me up, ever since! I enjoy writing poetry and drama, usually about emotional, humanitarian and philosophical issues. I am a member of the Outlanders and this is the first time I've been published.

Nawal Gadalla
Aquarian. 1954 Chinese horoscope horse of the year show-off. Anglo-Egyptian. (Thelwell pony posing as Arabic thoroughbred.) I like to play a drum, watch British soap operas, eat, and write funny things. 1985 stumbled upon Life Path teaching circle (or sacred) dance. 1986 found another Aquarian horse for stable companionship. Do I get the job?

Cora Greenhill
I live in a wooded valley in Derbyshire with my cat, three chickens and lots of vegetables, all of which inspire my writing. I love inner and outer journeying, exploring places sacred to the Goddess, dancing, and my work with women in Sheffield as a therapist and teacher. Last year I self-published my own collection of poems, *Dreadful Work*. I am forty-two, bisexual, have a teenage son, and am working on my first novel.

Toby Manning
Born in Manchester, brought up in North Wales. I've lived in Kent, Avon, Newcastle, and returned to Manchester in 1988. I've been writing seriously since 1988 and working as a freelance journalist for publications such as *Scene Out*, *The Pink Paper* and *City Life*. This will be my first published poetry and my last as I'm now concentrating on prose writing.

Monika Montsho
I am a Black working-class lesbian, am proud of that fact and hope that I never get old! I have great difficulty in being able to 'fit in' anywhere as my 'credentials' put me in a rather 'endangered species' group. My poetry is often 'sad, depressing, morbid' for which I make no apologies, as it simply reflects my experience of the world.

Russell Morris

I teach part time in further education which takes care of the food and bills and leaves the rest of my time free to paint and write. I use creativity as a means to make sense out of life to understand myself, others and the world at large.

Helen Smith

The slugs seemed made for, and were, the start of my writing poetry; 'Skin on Skin' is still my favourite poem. I am a member of the Outlanders, the lesbian writers' group, from which I draw inspiration and encouragement. At the moment I am working on a novel.

Christopher Watt

I was born and brought up in the West Riding of Yorkshire, where my parents were both Health Service managers. Aged twenty-one, I am a recent English graduate from Hull University. Presently I am taking a postgraduate course in Manchester and spend a lot of my time commuting between Manchester, and Hull, where I live with my partner.

Di Williams

I grew up in Manchester, feeling a misfit. In the '70s I discovered the Women's Movement and the Gay Liberation Front, which cheered me immensely. In the '80s I met increasing numbers of writers with whom I found common ground, and have been involved in workshops, both with women writers and mixed-gender (if that is a fair way to describe Northern Gay Writers). In the '90s I'm a survivor and actually like being here in Manchester.

Pat Winslow

I am thirty-five and live in Bolton with my ex-lover and three cats. Formerly an actor, I began writing only two and a half years ago. Too many white, male, heterosexual scripts had taken their toll. Now I run a writing group in Collyhurst and am working on my first novel instead.

About Commonword

Commonword is a non-profitmaking community publishing co-operative, producing books by writers in the North West, and supporting and developing their work. In this way Commonword brings new writing to a wide audience.

Over a period of ten years Commonword has published poetry, short stories and other forms of creative writing. *Beyond Paradise* is the eighth title to be published under the **Crocus** imprint.

In general, Commonword seeks to encourage the creative writing and publishing of the diverse groups in society who have lacked, or been excluded from, the means of expression through the written word. Working-class writers, black writers, women, and lesbians and gay men all too often fall into this category.

To give writers the opportunity to develop their work in an informal setting, Commonword offers a variety of writers' workshops, such as Womanswrite, the Monday Night Group, and Northern Gay Writers.

Cultureword which is a part of Commonword, and which acts as a focus for Asian and Afro-Caribbean writers, organises the Identity Writers' Workshop. Cultureword also co-ordinates 'Identity' magazine, and a writing competition for Black writers.

In addition to writers' workshops and publishing, Commonword offers a manuscript reading service to give constructive criticism, and can give information and advice to writers about facilities in their immediate locality.

Commonword is supported by: the Association of Greater Manchester Authorities, North West Arts and Manchester Education Committee.

The Commonword/Cultureword offices are at Cheetwood House, 21 Newton Street, Piccadilly, Manchester. Our phone number is (061) 236 2773. We would like to hear from you.

If you've enjoyed reading *Beyond Paradise*, why not try some of our other recent books?

Relative to Me...
Families are a subject we can all relate to, and the fictional stories in *Relative to Me...* touch us all with pieces that are funny, sad, and sometimes very moving. Stories move from Kanta Walker's Punjab in 'The Spilt Blood and The Sun' to the Maine Road Manchester City ground of 1934, as described by the characters of Tony Glynn's 'In Business'. The twenty stories in *Relative to Me...* capture the essence of family life in all its unpredictability.
£3.95   164 pages   ISBN 0 946745 70 6

No Earthly Reason?
The poems in *No Earthly Reason?* demonstrate a great concern for the environment — and a love of its beauty — shared by so many. Thirty-one poets present a remarkable variety of work; from Cath Staincliffe's lyrical description of seeing the earth from space to Mark Abraham's 'The Rime of the Savage Goldfish' — a hilarious spoof with a serious message. Each poet has a distinctive individual talent, and all are united by a common aim: the preservation of the planet — and its people!
"This beautiful book is a collection of reflections from the heart." Toyah Willcox
£3.50   100 pages   ISBN 0 946745 65 X

Talkers Through Dream Doors
Fourteen talented Black women write about their lives in *Talkers Through Dream Doors*, a collection of poetry and short stories. Through anger, laughter, and gentle reflection, they show us the world as they see it. Each expresses their identity in a distinctive and memorable style — from the cosmopolitan observations of Cindy Artiste to Jolina Black's down to earth humour in 'Ebony Baby Girl'. This collection is often moving, sometimes shocking, and it constantly presents an affirmation of the strength and creativity of Black women writers today.

*"The full potential of Black women writers has not yet been realised. A book like **Talkers Through Dream Doors** can only aid the process, and with such high standards, these women are going to spearhead the campaign." Caribbean Times*

£3.50   120 pages   ISBN 0 946745 60 9

Now Then

This new collection of poetry and short stories looks at lifestyles, work and leisure from 1945 to the present day. In 'Home For Whitsun' Elsie Maskell recalls the spectacle and excitement of the Salford Whit Walks. Ron Redshaw relives his comical boyhood adventures down by the river in 'Going Back On The Irwell'. Change and continuity is looked at humorously by Maureen Tottoh in 'For Judy', as she compares the fashions of then and now. For other writers it is their experiences of the world of work that remain the most vivid, as Nell Harwood depicts in 'It's My Life Isn't It?' These are just a small selection from the writing contained in *Now Then* which powerfully evokes the flavour of a crucial period in recent history.

"This book gives a vivid account of a host of changes... sometimes funny, sometimes cynical, the authors give a down-to-earth view of Northern working-class life." Oldham Evening Chronicle

£3.50   108 pages   ISBN 0 946745 55 2

She Says

She Says is a new collection from five women writers celebrating the vitality and variety of women's poetry today. Pat Amick writes movingly and skilfully about her feelings for her father, of childhood joys and of the bitter-sweet nature of romance. Cathy Bolton's work deals with relationships, and the way in which they are constantly cut across by questions of power, the past and sexuality. Anne Paley's poetry has a searching and reflective quality, whilst describing situations that affect many women. Sheila Parry uses powerful images, culled from folklore, myths and fairytales, in her work, whilst Cath Staincliffe expresses her thoughts about love, motherhood and politics in a way that is always challenging and original.

"This collection of poems is rich and varied in form and content and always thought provoking. Read it." 7 DAYS
£2.95   96 pages   ISBN 0 946745 50 1

Autobiography

Australian Journal: Alf Ironmonger   60p
In 1946, off the coast of South Australia, two young shipmates decide to jump ashore. This is their tale...
ISBN 0 946745 01 3   64 pages

Dobroyed: Leslie Wilson   £1.20
The unique inside story of one person's experience of a year spent in an approved school.
ISBN 0 950599 74 3   142 pages

Fiction

Holding Out: Short stories by women   £3.50
Women's lives are portrayed with realism, frankness and fun in this excellent collection of twenty-one short stories.
ISBN 0 946745 30 7   156 pages

Marshall's Big Score: John Gowling   £1.20
A book about a love affair, played out against the backdrop of the gay scene in London, Liverpool and Manchester.
ISBN 0 946745 03 X   76 pages

Turning Points: Northern Gay Writers   £2.95
This collection of short stories and poetry explores moments of crisis — turning points — in the lives of a variety of characters, with various different conclusions...
ISBN 0 946745 20 X   120 pages

Poetry

Black and Priceless   £3.50
"These words come from a generation who have no real voice in the society...the historians of the future shall have to relate to them if they are to obtain an insight into Black British life..." Benjamin Zephaniah
ISBN 0 946745 45 5   200 pages

Poetic Licence   £2.50
Poetic Licence is an exuberant and bubbling brew of poetry
from a diversity of poets living and working in Greater
Manchester. Their work celebrates the many pleasures of
poetry from the serious and intense, to the playful and
humorous.
ISBN 0 946745 40 4   208 pages

Between Mondays: The Monday Night Group   £2.50
This collection of poetry is the latest book from
Commonword's Monday Night Group. It brings together
some promising new writers with plenty to say about life
in the city, sexuality, Catholicism and many other subjects.
ISBN 0 946745 35 8   104 pages

Liberation Soldier: Joe Smythe   £2.50
Employing a variety of styles, Joe explores the discontents
and disturbances of the times, from inner city riots to
apartheid in South Africa.
ISBN 0 946745 25 0   84 pages

Hermit Crab: Di Williams   30p
Using the imagery of the sea and the seashore, these poems
tell of a daughter's journey towards independence.
ISBN 0 946745 15 3   28 pages

Consider Only This: Sarah Ward   30p
A selection of poems which captures the atmosphere of
moorland, cotton mills and small town life.
ISBN 0 946745 04 8   28 pages

Diary of A Divorce: Wendy Whitfield   £1.00
Wendy Whitfield reflects on the breakdown of her marriage
in a series of poems and cartoons.
ISBN 0 9505997 7 8   28 pages

ORDER FORM

TITLE	QUANTITY	PRICE	AMOUNT
Relative to Me...		£3.95	
Beyond Paradise		£4.50	
No Earthly Reason?		£3.50	
Talkers Through Dream Doors		£3.50	
Now Then		£3.50	
She Says		£2.95	
Black and Priceless		£3.50	
Holding Out		£3.50	
Poetic Licence		£2.50	
Between Mondays		£2.50	
Liberation Soldier		£2.50	
Turning Points		£2.95	
Hermit Crab		£0.30	
Consider Only This		£0.30	
Marshall's Big Score		£1.20	
Dobroyed		£1.20	
Australian Journal		£0.60	
Diary of A Divorce		£1.00	
		TOTAL	

Please send a cheque or postal order, made payable to Commonword Ltd, covering the purchase price plus 25p per book postage and packing.

NAME: ....

ADDRESS: ....

....

.... Postcode ....

Please return to: Commonword, Cheetwood House, 21 Newton Street, Manchester M1 1FZ.